The Aussie Slang Dictionary

About the Author

John Blackman is known to millions of Australians as 'The Voice' of **Hey Hey It's Saturday**, a highly successful, anarchic, ad-lib, weekly variety show networked across Australia through more than 144 television stations.

This 43-year-old entertainer, married with a teenage daughter, has delighted, shocked, amused and annoyed television and radio audiences for over twenty years. He has been described as witty, sharp, sexist and sardonic but always humorous and never boring.

Blackman has also endeared himself to television audiences through his many appearances on shows such as **The Paul Hogan Comedy Specials, Blankety Blanks, Family Feud, Personality Squares**, many commercials, numerous **Tonight** shows and small character roles in various soap operas. His radio **Breakfast Show** commands a huge listenership.

After months and months of nagging and badgering from his long-suffering wife and business partner, Cecile, Blackman finally succumbed and agreed to compile *The Aussie Slang Dictionary*, in which he reflects his cheeky, cynical sense of humour, while detailing some of the strange complexities of Australian colloquialisms.

Where words are inadequate, brilliant young cartoonist Andrew Fyfe has filled the gaps.

We know you will have as much fun reading this book as we had putting it together.

The Aussie Slang Dictionary

For Old and New Australians

Copyright text and illustrations © John Blackman Pty Ltd 1990

First published 1990 by Sun Books
THE MACMILLAN COMPANY OF AUSTRALIA PTY LTD
107 Moray Street, South Melbourne 3205
6 Clarke Street, Crows Nest 2065

Associated companies and representatives
throughout the world

National Library of Australia
cataloguing in publication data

Blackman, John.
   The Aussie slang dictionary for old and new Australians.
   ISBN 0 7251 0604 2.

   1. English language – Australia – Slang – Humor. I.
   Fyfe, Andrew. II. Title.
427.9940207

Set in Souvenir Light condensed and Souvenir Demi bold
Printed in Hong Kong

Pronunciation Guidelines

First, in order to develop a fair dinkum Australian accent, try not to open your mouth too widely when speaking and try talking through your nose. Accents tend to vary from state to state, but are generally similar, except as you move north where, due to the heat, folk tend to move and talk a lot more slowly.

You will note throughout this dictionary that we have a penchant for shortening words and names by adding an *ie*, an *o* or a *y* at the end. For example, if your name is Smith, you immediately become Smithy, a *musician* becomes a *muso* and *breakfast* becomes *brekkie*. Indeed, to some of my friends I am known as Blackie! This quaint practice serves to informalise our language and makes longer words easier to say.

Furthermore, *a* is generally sounded like *i*. Thus a *tailor* to your ears will sound very much like *tiler*. However, our *i* tends to come out as *oye*, which means your roof *tiler* has become a *toyler*. Getting the idea?

Most words with a *t* or double *t* are very often pronounced as *d*. For example, *little* becomes *liddle* and *title* becomes *tidal*.

Australians hardly ever emphasise *er* at the end of a word because, for some reason, *ah* is easier. For example, *beer* is *bee-ah*, *weather* is *weath-ah*, etc.

Also, the letter *h* is frequently pronounced as *haitch*, with the emphasis on the *h*, but when it has to be pronounced at the beginning of a word 'ere, we drop it!

Droppin' the *g* at the end of *-ing* words is almost compulsory.

Another odd way of shortening words is to drop a few letters and so *government* becomes *gumment* and *delinquent* becomes *delink*. Not content with that, some words are inexplicably lengthened, such as *new*, which is turned into two syllables and becomes *knee-yew*. For instance, a *nuclear* war becomes a *knee-yew-cle-ah* war. Still, if it does happen, who's gunna give a stuff how you pronounce it!

Finally, the letter *l* is hardly ever pronounced after a vowel and so Australia becomes *Uh-stray-ee-ya*! ... it's no wonder we say Aussie, Oz and Downunder. It's easier!

There are many other quirks in our language that are far too numerous to elaborate here, but the foregoing is a start ... GOOD LUCK!

aggro

A

If you dismiss someone out-of-hand, you are said to have given them the 'big A'. It stands for 'arse', which Americans call 'ass'.

act the goat

To behave in a silly or foolish manner.

aggro

Abbreviation of 'aggravation'. If a person is a bit aggro, they are more than a little cross and looking for an argument or a fight.

airs

Abbreviation of the phrase 'airs and graces'. If you put on airs and graces you are being just a little pretentious ... Pretentious, moi?

airy-fairy

Something of very little substance.

Akubra

Broad-brimmed Australian bush hat made from rabbit fur.

Akubra

Al Capone

Rhyming slang for 'telephone'. 'Eau de Cologne' is also frequently used for same . . . so you can give someone a gin sling (ring)!

Alice

Abbreviation for 'The Alice' which is an abbreviation for Alice Springs, a small town in the Northern Territory not far from Ayers Rock, the world's largest monolith.

alkie

Abbreviation for an alcoholic.

all right

Phrase often used to indicate everything's okay. Occasionally pronounced 'orright' . . . Orright!?

ankle biter

Young child, sometimes referred to as a 'rug rat'.

ankle biter

ants' pants

If something is the ants' pants it is generally the height of fashion. If you think *you* are the ants' pants, you are said to have an unreasonably high opinion of yourself.

Anzac

An Australian soldier. Derived from the armed forces during World War I, the Australian and New Zealand Army Corps. You remember World War I? That was the one they fought in black and white!

apples

Used in the phrase 'She'll be apples!' meaning everything will be okay.

appro

If you have something 'on appro' (approval) you are inspecting that article before you feel obligated to buy.

Aristotle

Rhyming slang for 'bottle' . . . usually full of beer.

arty farty

Very pretentious or snobbish.

arty farty

arvo   Abbreviation for 'afternoon'. 'See ya this arvo!'

Aussie   Australian ... y'know, just like Paul Hogan.

Aussie Rules   Football game, sometimes referred to by 'knockers' as 'aerial ping pong', because the ball is often kicked high into the air, requiring players to leap and catch it. The Grand Final in Melbourne each September attracts almost 100 000 spectators! 'Carn the Mighty Lions!' ... (primitive Aussie footy chant).

she'll be apples

Australian salute   The constant movement of one's hand required to brush away the ever-present blowfly.

axe handle   Primitive unit of measurement. 'He was a big bloke ... about ten axe handles across!' means he was very broad-shouldered.

ay?   A word used when you didn't quite catch what somebody said ... Pardon?

HAWTHORN SECONDARY COLLEGE
BURGESS STREET
EAST HAWTHORN, 3123

bag

backchat	Answering back in an impertinent manner.
back o'beyond	As far out in the bush as one could possibly get, often used in reference to the outback.
bag	Uncomplimentary term for a woman. Wives are sometimes referred to as 'the old bag' (except mine of course!).
bagging	The act of criticising someone or something quite severely. Film critics, for instance, often give a bad movie a 'good bagging' ... which is a bit of a contradiction in terms.
bag of fruit	Rhyming slang for a man's suit.
balls-up	Term used for something that has gone terribly wrong: 'It was a terrible balls-up', means it was a total screw-up!

banana bender — Anyone who lives in the Australian state of Queensland (where most of our bananas are grown). The problem is they don't have any left because they keep throwing away all the bent ones!

bananas — If you go bananas, you have become really angry. Either that, or you're mentally unstable . . . which is not very a-peeling! BOO!

banged-up — Pregnant . . . yes, but is she sure she's the mother!?

bang-on — Expression which means absolutely correct, dead centre, well done or bull's eye!

barbie — Abbreviation of barbecue, cook-out. A person who is mentally deficient is said to be 'one steak short of a barbie' or, if you like, 'two sandwiches short of a picnic'.

barbie

barge in (to)   To force one's way into a conversation or company or to collide with something.

barney   A fight or an argument. We'll clear away the 'rubble' later! (Apologies to Fred, Wilma and Betty!)

barrack   To cheer and shout in support of your team. (As in 'rooting', in the U.S.A.)

bash (1)   A party or a celebration.

bash (2)   To thump verbally. In Australia, our favourite 'bashees' include unions, tall poppies, doctors, social climbers, politicians, entrepreneurs or anyone else who rises above the pack.

bash, give it a   To try one's hand at something. 'I think I'll give it a bash.'

basket case   Somebody who is in a state of mental exhaustion and on the brink of collapse.

basket case

bat

Yet another uncomplimentary term for a woman. She's so ugly, you look up the word in the dictionary and there's a photo of her!

bat and ball

Rhyming slang for 'wall'. Also, for 'stall' as when you 'bat and ball' your car.

batching

Term used for men who have to look after themselves while their wives are away. Derived from 'bachelor'.

bat out of hell

If someone is moving at great speed they are said to be moving like a 'bat out of hell'. This amazing phenomenon is observed in factories and offices all over Australia just before lunch, or around 4.30 p.m. on a Friday afternoon.

bathers

Swimming trunks.

battler

Somebody who works very hard against insurmountable odds but never seems to get anywhere. Working-class Australians are known as 'little Aussie battlers'.

B.B.Q.

Yet another abbreviation for barbecue.

beak

A person's nose. 'He doesn't really have a big beak, it's just that his face is too small.'

beauty

An exclamation of approval. Variations include: 'Beaut!', 'Bewdy bottler!', 'Bewdy!'

beddy-byes

A juvenile term for bed-time.

bell

If you give someone a bell, it means you call them on the telephone.

belt

If you give someone a belt, it's not to hold their trousers up ... you have just punched them! If you punch them continuously, they are said to have received a 'belting'!

betcha A lazy way of saying 'Bet you!', e.g. 'Betcha can't run a mile in three minutes!'. Do not take this bet with Carl Lewis!

better half Generally one's wife or husband. My wife and I started out with nothing . . . and we've got most of it left!

bib and tucker Term used to describe clothes. 'She was dressed in her best bib and tucker.'

bible basher Generally a person of Christian persuasion . . . they invariably try to ram their convictions down your throat!

big note If you 'big note' yourself, you are making yourself more important than you really are.

big sticks Term used for goal-posts in Aussie Rules football. If a player boots the ball through them he has kicked a goal . . . 'He's put it through the big sticks!'

bikkie Childish abbreviation for 'biscuit', and also used to mean money. If a person is making a lot of money, they are said to be making 'big bikkies'. Of course, they started out on crummy salaries! BOO!

billy A tin can with a wire handle generally suspended over a camp-fire for the purpose of boiling water to make tea.

billy lid Rhyming slang for kid (young child) . . . *not* to be suspended over a camp-fire unless he or she has a wire handle.

billy-oh A non-existent place you tell somebody you don't like to go to! In effect, by telling them to go to 'billy-oh', you are telling them to get lost.

billy

bingle

Australian expression for a minor car smash. 'George had a bingle in his car last night!' ... Like the drunk who ran into a police car: the cop says, 'Didn't you see me?' The drunk says, 'I hit you didn't I?'

bite

Not something a dog does ... someone who 'puts the bite' on you is generally asking you to lend them some money.

bitzer

A dog of mixed parentage. Also referred to as a mongrel (pronounced mung-grol).

bizzo

Abbreviation for business in the most general sense. 'At school we learned about maths, science and all that bizzo!'

Black Stump

Non-existent part of Australia alleged to be right in the centre of the continent. 'She makes the best cakes this side of the Black Stump!' ... Come to think of it, they *taste* a bit like the Black Stump!

blazes

No, not a series of fires but yet another mythical, non-existent place to tell someone you don't like to go to! 'Go to blazes!' means, once again, 'Get lost!'

blimey

An exclamation of surprise, sometimes lengthened to 'Blimey Teddy!'

bloke

A complimentary term for the average Australian male and usually preceded by the adjectives 'good', 'nice' or 'fair dinkum'.

bloody

Commonly known as the Great Australian Adjective. It is often used to emphasise either approval or disapproval. 'That's a bloody lovely car!' or 'What a terrible bloody game that was!' Bloody good adjective that!

bloody oath

An exclamation of total agreement with something. 'Do you like beer?' . . . 'Bloody oath I do!' Hey, let's stop all this bloody swearing and move on to the next bloody word!

blow in

If you blow in on someone, you have just paid them an unexpected visit.

blow through

If you do this, you have left very quickly without having said goodbye or settled any unfinished business.

bludge

A person who doesn't work and lives off the toils of others is said to be having a bludge. We don't like bludgers in Australia. However, if it's your day off work, it is quite acceptable to do nothing all day and bludge around the house . . . confusing isn't it?

blue (1)

A fight or an argument. 'Harry got into a bit of a blue (fight) with another bloke at the football yesterday. And, to top things off, he went home and had a blue (argument) with his missus!' . . . even more confusing!

bludge

Blue (2)   For some strange reason, anybody who has red hair is referred to as 'Blue' in Australia.

bluey (1)   A rolled-up blanket generally containing a wandering bushman's worldly possessions. To 'hump one's bluey' is not the deviant act you think it is. To 'hump' means to carry something on your back, which is what a bushman does with his bluey!

bluey (2)   A subpoena to appear in court, so called because these summonses are generally printed on blue paper.

bob

Old slang term for what is now our ten-cent coin. Prior to 1966, a bob was known as a shilling. The term is still in use today ... if somebody is rich, they are said to 'have a few bob'. I personally have enough money to last me the rest of my life, provided I die tomorrow!

bob's your uncle

An expression used to indicate that you totally understand a situation. A wise guy will sometimes reply, 'Yeah, and Fanny's your aunt!' Quaint, isn't it?

bodgie

If an item is said to be bodgie, either it's stolen or it is extremely deficient in quality.

bomb

An old car. 'The car he's driving is a bit of a bomb, but it goes okay.' ... Don't worry about the smoke coming out from the hood ... it was once owned by the Pope.

bonzer

If something is bonzer, it is really very pleasing. A bonzer bloke is someone who can be trusted and is a 'good sport' all round.

boot (1)

Not only something you wear on your feet, but something that happens when you get fired from a job. 'Poor old George got the boot yesterday.' ... They couldn't afford to give him a gold watch, but they do ring him each morning to tell him the time!

boot (2)

Australian and British expression for car trunk.

boozer

Pub. When you're off to the boozer, what you really mean is that you're off to the pub for a drink!

booze-up

The act of indulging in a prolonged bout of drinking. Occasionally, a drunken party is referred to as a booze-up ... generally attended by boozers!

bo-peep

bo-peep	Sorry, nothing to do with sheep! It means to have a sly look at something. 'Take a bo-peep at that, will ya!'
bot	When you're on the bot, you're generally down on your luck and asking someone for money or a cigarette. 'Excuse me, mate, I couldn't bot (bum) a fag (cigarette) could I?' If you indulge in this practice long enough, you become known as a botter or a bludger ... which reminds me ... 'Hi!' to my brother-in-law!
bottler	A term used to express delight. 'You little bottler!'
brasco	Slang term for toilet.
breadbasket	If a boxer is hit in the breadbasket, of course he's just been hit in the stomach! My father was a boxer ... my mother was a labrador. (GROAN!)
brekkie	Yet another example of the Australian penchant for shortening words and putting 'ie' on the end. Did you get breakfast? Very clever! You may leave the prunes.

brick

If a chap is a real brick, he is totally honest, reliable and trustworthy. (I could have sworn I said brick!)

bucket

Not something you carry water in, but something you do when you soundly criticise something or someone. In other words, they have just been bucketed or had a bucket tipped on them ... We like to bucket politicians frequently! In fact, we like to make statues of them and let the pigeons speak for us all!

bucks' night

A party thrown the night before a bloke gets married. Traditionally, his mates endeavour to make him so ill, the poor guy barely makes it up the aisle the next day ... great fun eh? I remember my bucks' night vividly ... Dad still can't figure out how we got his car into the sauna!

bugger off

Get lost, scram!

bugle

Another euphemism for the nose. If something in your fridge is a 'bit on the bugle', it means it's a bit smelly and should be thrown out. Judging from the smell coming from ours, the *fridge* should be thrown out!

bull

If someone is talking a lot of nonsense, they are talking a lot of bull. Generally, if an Aussie bloke doesn't agree with what you're saying, he'll probably declare the argument closed with a shout of 'Bulldust!' Anyone who speaks a load of bull is generally referred to as a bulldust artist.

bullet

Another way you can be fired from your job in Australia is to 'cop the bullet' ... unless of course, you're a human cannonball in a circus ... in which case you get fired *every* day!

bum

In America, a bum is either a tramp or something you do when you ask someone for a cigarette. In Australia, it's neither ... it's what we sit on! I'm glad we got to the bottom of that one!

bumfreezer   You don't have to be Einstein to figure out that it's a very short jacket!

bunch of fives   If an Aussie bloke offers you a bunch of fives, you'd better duck! What he wants to do is punch you ... a bunch of fives is his fist! Sometimes known as a knuckle sandwich ... hold the mayo!

bung   Basically, this word simply means 'put'. For instance, you can bung a cake in the oven; bung on side (pretend you are a lot cleverer than you really are); bung on an act (John McEnroe has made an art form of this). When you've finished reading this little tome, why don't you bung it on your bookshelf!?

bumfreezer

bunghole   Slang for cheese ... self-explanatory when you realise what cheese can do to you (and you break up the syllables!)

burl   If you give something a burl, you give it a try. But if a car is burling down the street, it is going pretty fast. Indeed, when you test drive a car you are buying, you generally take it for a burl around the block!

butchers (1)

If one is feeling a little 'butchers', one is feeling a little ill. 'Butchers' is the abbreviation of 'butcher's hook' which is rhyming slang for 'crook' which means not well. Simple really, when you think about it!

butchers (2)

Now, this is a little easier. An Aussie who invites you to take a 'butchers' at some snapshots is inviting you to take a 'look' ... and so we're back to 'butcher's hook' again!

bye-bye

A form of saying goodbye. It is also used in an infantile sense when one is going to sleep ... little Johnny has gone 'bye-byes' ... nauseating, huh?

B.Y.O (verb)

If you go to a party or restaurant and you are requested to B.Y.O., it simply means you are required to bring your own liquor. Many restaurants in Australia do not have a licence to sell liquor on their premises, but it is quite legal to B.Y.O. ... okay?

chunder

cackle berry

Not something that grows on a tree but simply an egg. The cackle of course comes from the sound the chook makes when she lays it. What's a chook? Read on!

cactus

If an item becomes totally useless it is said to be 'cactus'. Also, if someone dies or has a terminal disease, they are said to be cactus. Children are cactus when they are prickly and hard to get along with.

cakehole

The mouth.

camp

In Australia, as in the U.S.A., camp is somewhere you can send your kids for their holidays. However, be very careful not to call a bloke 'camp' because you have just implied he's a homosexual!

cactus

cancer stick   A cigarette.

Captain Cook   Rhyming slang for 'look'. Often shortened to 'Captains'. Captain Cook, incidentally, was the discoverer of this great country over two hundred years ago. He was later killed by the natives of the then Sandwich Islands. Ever been speared in the Sandwiches? Certainly make your eyes water. OUCH!

carbie   An abbreviation of carburettor. For the average Australian petrol-head, the more triple-throated, the better.

cardie   Short for cardigan.

cark   If someone has 'carked it' they have died. As a matter of fact, they are totally cactus!

c'arn
Shortened version of 'Come on!'. Used mainly when barracking for one's team: 'C'arn the mighty Lions!!'

case
Someone who is a little strange and eccentric. 'That bloke's a real case!' A 'hopeless case', of course, is a dozen empty beer bottles!

cert
If someone at the race-track tells you a horse is a dead cert to win the race, put the rent on it ... it's a cert-ainty!

charlie
Shortened rhyming slang for Charlie Wheeler ... sheila ... meaning a woman. See? It does get easier doesn't it!

cheerio
Form of saying good-bye.

cherry
Term for brand new cricket ball ... very red and shiny!

chewie
Here we go again ... shortening words and bunging 'ie' on the end. If you got 'chewing gum' give yourself a pat on the back!

chinwag
A good, long chat.

chippie
Because they spend most of their time chipping away at bits of wood, we call carpenters chippies.

chock-a-block
Absolutely full. 'The train was chock-a-block with passengers.' 'Chockers' is also frequently used.

choof off
A person who is about to choof off is about to leave your company (as in a train choofing off from a station).

chook
A chicken, hen or rooster.

Chrissie
You guessed it ... yet another slang obscenity. Chrissie is what a lot of us call Christmas!

chuck (1)   Generally something we do with a ball ... we don't throw it, we chuck it!

chuck (2)   Generally something we do if we've eaten too much ... we don't throw up — we chuck!

chunder   Exactly the same as 'chuck' (2).

ciggie   Good, now you're getting the idea! A cigarette!

clackers   Dentures ... remember, always be true to your teeth and they'll never be false to you!

clanger   Something one drops, just like a faux pas. 'Joe dropped a real clanger when he took his clackers out in front of the Queen!'

clapped   Term used to indicate that something has outlived its usefulness. 'Jane's car is totally clapped out.'

clappers   If your car goes really fast, it is said to 'go like the clappers'.

clip   A mild form of punishment dealt with the open hand. 'His mother gave him a clip under the ear.'

clobber (1)   If you clobber someone, it means you have just assaulted them.

clobber (2)   An outfit of clothing. 'Say Bill, that's a lovely set of clobber you've got on!'

clout   Very similar to 'clip' ... only it hurts a bit more!

cobber   Good old Aussie expression for a pal or friend.

cock-and-bull   If someone tells you a cock-and-bull story, they have probably told a story that is totally untrue. 'Sounds like a whole lot of cock-and-bull to me!'

cock-up   A terrible mess that has gone dreadfully wrong. Very similar to a balls-up or a screw-up.

cocky (1)   Abbreviation of a cockatoo or parrot.

cocky (2)   A word used to describe farmers or small land-owners. Embellishments to this word sometimes include 'cow cocky', 'fruit cocky', 'cane cocky', 'sheep cocky' and so on.

codger   Generally speaking, a codger is an elderly gentleman.

codger

cods   Euphemism for testicles. 'Poor old Wilbur was kicked right in the cods.'

codswallop   Absolute nonsense.

coffin nail   A cigarette.

coldie   Term used for a cold can of beer.

collywobbles   When you have an upset stomach, you are said to have the dreaded collywobbles!

comic cuts   Rhyming slang for that area known as your stomach or guts. 'He punched him right in the comics!'

conchie   Anyone who is conscientious is known as being conchie.

conk   Yet another term for nose.

conk out   If your car breaks down it conks out!

cooee   A loud call used in the bush to attract attention. If you're 'within cooee' of something, you're close to it.

copper   Exactly the same as a cop ... except this time we didn't shorten it!

cop shop   A police station.

corker   If you are having a corker of a time you're really enjoying yourself.

cossie   A swimming costume.

cot case   Anyone who drinks to the point where all they can do is crash into bed is regarded as a cot case.

cove   Another term for a man. 'He was a gentle sort of cove.'

crack   An Aussie who cracks a tinnie has just opened a can of beer ... cheers!

crackers   No, not something you dip into your soup. Someone who goes crackers has gone insane. (Must have been from eating all those crackers!)

crawler   A despicable sycophant who is full of insincere flattery.

cracking a tinnie

creamed

If your team has just won a game by 500 points, it would be safe to say they creamed the opposition.

cricket

Very complicated bat and ball game invented by the English. Some matches (Tests) are played between Australia and another country over five days and finish in a draw. We revere our cricketers in much the same way that Americans worship their champion baseball players. To give you an idea of just how complex the game of cricket is, here is an attempt at a simple explanation:

There are two sides each consisting of eleven players. One side sends the other side in to bat until they are all out, then the other side goes in till they're all out. Whoever makes the most runs wins, unless the match can't be finished within time in which case neither side wins and it's declared a draw. Personally, I think it would be easier if you came to Australia and watched a game (that's if you've got five days to spare). If you haven't, we do have one-day matches which take about seven hours to complete. Owzat!?

crikey

An expression of surprise.

cripes

A similar expression of surprise.

crook

If you are not feeling very well, you are feeling crook.

crow-eater

Term used to describe a resident of the state of South Australia ... please don't ask me why.

cuppa

Abbreviation for 'cup of tea'. 'Let's sit down for a minute and have a cuppa.'

curry

When you give someone a bit of curry, you have in effect abused that person quite angrily.

dunny

Dad 'n' Dave   Rhyming slang for shave. These legendary characters feature in Steele Rudd's famous book *On Our Selection*.

dag   Anybody who is a little eccentric or even stupid is regarded as a bit of a dag.

daisy-cutter   A sports term for any ball that skims just above the grass after being chucked (sorry, thrown), hit or kicked.

daks   Another name for trousers.

damper   Primitive form of bread, made in the bush from flour and water and cooked on the coals of a camp-fire.

dag

Dead Heart — That region of Australia situated in the middle of the arid Northern Territory ... so called because nothing much grows there!

dead marine — The most forlorn sight a typical Aussie boozer ever sees ... an empty beer bottle.

demo — If you want to protest about the government's policies, you stage a demo (demonstration) ... well, it is a very long word and it does have four syllables!

derro — The Australian equivalent of wino. Short, of course, for 'derelict'.

devo — Abbreviation for 'deviant'.

dickhead — Popular Aussie expression of scorn for anyone who behaves in an idiotic or foolish manner. Be very careful whom you address in this way as he may well be one and punch your lights out!

diddle — If you diddle someone, you actually swindle them.

dig — When you have a dig at someone, you are being sarcastic towards them.

digger — A term originally used to describe an Australian nineteenth-century goldminer and later used to typify the Australian soldier. These days, a very yuppie term when you can't remember someone's name at a cocktail party. However, 'G'day Digger', should not be used when meeting Royalty!

din-dins — I'm almost ashamed to say . . . childish expression for 'dinner'.

ding — Used to describe a small dent in a car. 'The front mudguard has a bit of a ding, but apart from that, it's unmarked.'

dink — When you carry someone on your bicycle you are giving them a dink.

dinki-di — See Fair Dinkum.

divvy — This quaint little word can mean dividend or, if you are splitting up some money, you are divvying it up. Or it could be that lump of turf you dislodge after a bad golf shot, commonly known as a divot.

dob (1) — To tattle-tale on someone is to dob them in. Don't ever be a dobber, and especially not a cobber-dobber . . . it's very un-Australian, orright?!

dob (2) — When a footballer kicks a goal, the ball is often described as having been dobbed. 'He's dobbed it right through the middle, folks!'

doco — Short documentary ... but you knew that didn't you?

dog's eye — Rhyming slang for that great Aussie repast—the meat pie. I'll have mine with a bit of dead horse (tomato sauce), thanks mate!

dole bludger — A person who makes no attempt to get a job and is content to live off Social Welfare payments.

dong — A hit or strike. 'He was donged on the head by a falling brick.'

donk (1) — An engine. 'That Chevrolet has a great donk under the hood.'

donk (2) — Euphemism for penis, or, for the faint at heart, 'tummy banana' or 'donger'.

dosh — Money!

drip — If a person is a drip, they are generally a pathetic, colourless, non-personality!

drongo — A dim-witted, slow person ... very similar to your average drip.

droob — Also very similar to your average drip and drongo ... the Aussie droob is a distant cousin of a nerd!

drop — The expression used when you fell someone. 'He dropped him with a beautiful upper-cut.'

drop your bundle — An expression used when one loses control of a situation and gives up. 'She was leading the tournament by ten strokes when she dropped her bundle on the seventh with a quadruple bogie.'

drover's dog — Someone of absolutely no importance. That's why my wife makes me sleep out in the toolshed some nights!

dubbo

Again, another euphemism for your average drip, drongo, droob or nerd. Also, the name of an Australian country town in the state of New South Wales ... it's not advisable to use this term in this town or you could get 'dropped'.

duck

A term used in our quaint game of cricket whenever a batsman is bowled out for no score. 'He's out for a duck!' ... I often score ducks at discos!

ducks and drakes

Rhyming slang for the 'shakes' ... generally brought on by a severe bout of drinking. I have a very bad drinking problem ... for one thing, I spill far too much!

duck's disease

An uncomplimentary way of alluding to a short person. His bum (ass) is too close to the ground You know, the sort of guy who goes deaf dancing with Dolly Parton.

drop

duds   Clothes, especially trousers or pants.

duffer (1)   Aussie expression for a cattle rustler.

duffer (2)   Yet another, but gentler, term for your average drip, drongo, droob and nerd ... and no, they are not a firm of attorneys!

dunny   Aussie expression for outdoor toilet not connected to any sewerage system and usually found some distance from the house ... mostly a small wooden shed with a wooden toilet seat placed on top of a large sanitary can.

dyke   Same as dunny.

Esky

earbasher	A very boring person who never stops talking.
eau de Cologne	Rhyming slang for 'telephone'.
egg beater	A term for 'helicopter', due to the fact that the rotor blades could be likened to the average domestic kitchen utensil . . . and they do 'whisk' you through the air!
elbow grease	Quaint term for hard work. If you are digging a large trench it requires quite a bit of elbow grease. Not available in department stores.
elephants	Shortened version of 'elephant's trunk', which is rhyming slang for drunk. 'I was so elephants last night, I turned a glass of milk into yoghurt just by breathing on it!'

earbasher

emma chisit   Not a famous Australian woman but our very lazy way of saying, 'How much is it?'

Esky   Trademarked name for a portable icebox or 'car fridge'. Found frequently at football or cricket matches ... ideal for putting your 'coldies' in or for standing on if you've got 'duck's disease'!

elbow grease

elephants

five-finger discount

face fungus — Any hair on your face such as a beard or moustache. I still remember sitting on that lap, stroking that long white beard ... Gee, I miss Grannie!

fag — Slang expression for cigarette. Also euphemism for gentlemen who prefer the company of other gentlemen.

fair dinkum — An interjection or question describing someone or something that is truly genuine or correct. 'It was a great game, fair dinkum!' 'Fair dinkum, was it?'

fair enough — 'Okay, you win! I don't agree with you ... but I don't want to have a blue!'

fang — If you fang somebody for a couple of dollars, you have just borrowed a couple of dollars ... Now, don't be a bludger and make sure you pay it back!

Farmer Giles	Rhyming slang for piles or hemorrhoids.
fat	If you are chewing the fat, it simply means you are talking.
fat chance	If you have no hope of becoming a multi-millionaire you have a fat chance ... This dictionary has a fat chance of winning a Pulitzer prize for literature!
fibber	Anyone who tells lies ... fibs.
five-finger discount	Anyone who has just indulged in a little shoplifting or stealing has just received this dubious reduction in price.
flake (1)	A long sleep induced by a prolonged bout of drinking or physical exercise. 'Last night I was so exhausted I flaked out before dinner!'
flake (2)	Another name for shark meat. A favourite Aussie meal, especially on Fridays, is flake and chips (fries).

fang

flaming

A favourite Australian adjective. 'We had a flaming good time last night!'

flat chat

If you drive a car to its maximum speed, it is said to be going at 'flat chat'.

flat out

Very similar to flat chat ... in fact almost the same speed.

flatties

Ladies' shoes with low heels.

flick

When something has outlived its usefulness you generally throw it away ... or, in Australia, you give it the flick.

flicks

The cinema, originally derived from the early days when movies would 'flicker' on the big screen. I take my wife to the drive-in movies every Friday night ... when the movie's over, I go back and pick her up!

flaking out

flipping

Used instead of that other 'F' word to express contempt or disgust. 'He's a flipping bore!'

floater

A meat pie floating in a bowl of pea soup. This delectable, sophisticated dish originated in the state of South Australia ... Quick-Eze anyone?

fluff

Quaint Aussie term for breaking wind ... (Must have been the 'floater'!)

fluke

A lucky break that happens purely by chance. 'I really fluked that hole-in-one!'

footie

Abbreviation for football. Pronounced 'foody'.

Fred Nerk

An Australian relative of John Doe. Generally used to describe an imaginary person.

freight

Euphemism for money. 'He took quite a bit of freight to the track and lost the lot!'

French letter

Term used to describe a condom.

frog and toad

Rhyming slang for 'road'.

front

If you have a lot of front, you are said to be brash, bold and totally unashamed. 'He's got more front than Myer!' ... Myer is a large department store in Melbourne.

full

Intoxicated. A favourite expression for someone who is totally inebriated is 'He was as full as a boot!'

fun bags

With the utmost respect, Dolly Parton would have the best set of these in the western world!

funny farm

Psychiatric hospital or mental institution.

goose

gab	To talk incessantly. My wife definitely has the gift of the gab . . . in fact, I haven't spoken to her for three years . . . I hate to interrupt!!
ga-ga	If you become besotted by something or someone, you are said to be ga-ga about it!
galah	An Australian parrot or a loud, rudely behaved person.
galoot	Very similar to our drip, drongo, droob and nerd!
game (as Ned Kelly)	Adventurous, foolhardy and willing to take a chance. As did the infamous bushranger, Ned Kelly, who wore a tin helmet with a slot for his eyes to see through. The last time I tried that somebody posted six letters in my face!

gander — No, not a male goose but what you do when you have a look at something . . . you take a gander!

garbo — Nothing to do with the great Greta, but someone who collects your garbage. The more refined rubbish collectors like to think of themselves as garbologists.

gasbag — Someone who talks a lot.

gay and hearty — Rhyming slang for party.

gazunder — Any of us who suffer nocturnal incontinence knows what this little item is. It's a potty and it 'gazunder' the bed!

g'day — Now that's an easy one . . . just ask Paul Hogan!

gee gee — Childish expression for horse.

ga-ga

goanna   Rhyming slang for piano.

goner   Anyone who is beyond help or dead. 'The tree fell right on top of him, Mrs Jones ... I'm afraid he's a goner.'

good nick   The exact opposite of poor Mrs Jones' hubby ... if something is in good nick, it's in very good condition.

good-oh   Slang equivalent of okay.

googy-egg   Infantile terminology for an egg.

goose (1)   Someone who is a bit silly.

goose (2)   Something you do to someone when you sneak up behind them and grab them between the buttocks. We're still not too sure who derives the most pleasure from this quaint activity ... the goosee or the goosor!

goose's neck   Rhyming slang for 'cheque', or you may use 'Gregory', as in Gregory Peck.

greaser   A sycophant ... very similar to a 'crawler'.

grizzle   Complain constantly. We often grizzle about the bad weather ... when we do we are referred to as a 'grizzleguts'.

grog   Our term for booze or alcohol. When you spend too much at the hotel drinking, you are in fact 'grogging on'!

grot   Dirt or filth. X-rated movies are often referred to as grotty, as is an unclean person.

grouse   Excellent, great, terrific, beaut, fantastic! I am married to a grouse sheila! ... She may read this book and it's always a good idea to grease to the missus!

greaser

grub	Very similar to your average grot.
gummies	Slang for gumboots, long rubber boots generally worn by farmers, etc.
gunner	A procrastinator ... someone who is forever gunner do this and gunner do that!
gurgler	A plughole. If something has failed, it is said to have 'gone down the gurgler'. I hope this book doesn't go down the gurgler!
gutser	If you 'come a gutser' you have just fallen over.
gyp	Swindle.

hoon

hey diddle diddle	Rhyming slang for 'piddle' (urinate).
highway robbery	The act of extracting an exorbitant amount of money for goods or services and getting next to nothing in return. See 'taxes'!
hoon	A show-off of limited ability and mental capacity.
hostie	Shortened version of 'air hostess'. Nowadays they like to be referred to as 'flight attendants'. Incidentally, we have some of the prettiest in the world . . . some of the women aren't bad either! Only jokin' chaps!!
howzat?	Loud appeal made to an umpire during a game of cricket to ascertain if a batsman is 'out' or not.

hostie

hum

If something is a bit smelly, it has a bit of a 'hum'.

hump

Oh you naughty thing! In Australia, hump means carry. In other words, you may hump wood in from the shed. Indeed, if your wife can't walk, it is permissible to hump her as well! ... even in public!

humpy

A mean bush dwelling.

highway robbery

howzat?

iffy

idiot box

Television set. So called because most of us sit in front of it for hours, wide-eyed and slack-jawed. I said to my wife the other night, 'Crikey, this is boring!' and she said, 'If you think this is boring, wait till I turn it *on*!'

iffy

If something is 'a bit iffy', it's suspect or risky ... and it's better not to be involved.

in like Flynn

A phrase indicating success in an enterprise or a sexual encounter. It originated from the legendary sexual prowess of Errol Flynn, the Australian-born actor who became famous in American movies. 'Is that a cutlass, or are you just glad to see me!?'

innings

Term used in the sport of cricket for the time spent batting. If you die at a ripe old age, you are said to have had a 'good innings'.

in like Flynn

Irish
Shortened version of 'Irish jig', which is rhyming slang for 'wig'. 'That's a nice undetectable Irish you're wearing, George!'

iron-out
Some men in Australia 'iron-out' as well as women, but it has nothing to do with flattening clothes ... It's other guys! It actually means knocking someone out.

irrits
If you give someone the 'irrits', it means you are being very irritating ... and it's a good time to shoot through.

ivories
The teeth.

ivories, to tickle
To play the piano.

irrits

ivories

jackeroo

Jack and Jill	Rhyming slang for 'bill'. If someone offers to pay your 'Jack 'n' Jill' at a restaurant . . . don't refuse!
jackeroo	Young apprentice stockman or cowboy, generally found on outback ranches. The female equivalent is known as a jilleroo.
jaw-breaker	A very hard-to-chew piece of candy, or a long unpronounceable word.
jerry	A chamber pot that 'gazunder' your bed each night in case you wake up and feel like a 'hey diddle diddle'.
jiffy	A short period of time. 'I'll be with you in a jiffy.'
jiggered	If something is jiggered, it is no longer useful. By the time I finish this dictionary, I'll be jiggered!

Jimmy Riddle   See 'hey diddle diddle'.

job   Something we should all have but, in Oz, it also means punch, as in 'If you keep saying those insulting things, I'll job you right on the nose!'

Joe Blake   Rhyming slang for snake ... sometimes referred to as 'Joeys'.

Joe Blakes   Rhyming slang for the 'shakes', generally brought on by a prolonged bout of boozing.

Joe Blow   General term for anybody who doesn't have a name. 'Any Joe Blow would tell you that!'

joey   A baby kangaroo carried around in its mother's pouch.

joker   Nothing to do with Batman but another term for a fellow. 'This joker came up to me and asked for a cigarette!'

jumbuck   Featured in our world-famous song, 'Waltzing Matilda', a 'jumbuck' is derived from an Aboriginal word for a sheep.

jumper   Australian word for sweater, or jersey.

jaw-breaker

jerry

kangaroo (that's *me*, stupid!)

kangaroo

Although these lovable creatures have become symbolic of Australia, in some areas they are regarded as vermin due to their large numbers. As such, anybody who is a bit crazy is said to 'keep kangaroos in the top paddock'.

kip (1)

A short nap.

kip (2)

The small piece of wood used in our famous game of two-up. The two coins are placed on the kip and then thrown into the air, with participants betting on whether the coins will come down heads or tails.

Kiwi

Any person who comes from New Zealand. A kiwi is a nocturnal New Zealand bird.

knackered

Absolutely exhausted or worn out.

Kiwi

knickers

Underpants or panties. Instead of saying 'keep your shirt on!', we say 'Don't get your knickers in a twist!'

knock

To knock something in Australia is to criticise it, and when you 'knock' something you become a knocker. Knockers, on the other hand, are something else again!

knock-back

If you cop a knock-back at a disco, it means a girl has turned you down.

knocking shop

A house of ill-repute.

knock-off time

Time to go home from your place of employment.

knock-up

If you've just knocked-up your girlfriend, it means you've just made her pregnant. I had a military wedding . . . well, put it this way . . . there were plenty of guns there!

knock-up

knotted, get

This mildly offensive phrase means 'Screw you!' Of course, I mean that in the nicest possible way.

knuckle sandwich

Quite simply a punch in the mouth ... with a bunch of fives.

knotted

L

lair

la de da	If you are perceived to be snobbish or pretentious you are said to be a bit 'la de da' ... Apologies to Dianne Keaton!
Lady (or Lord) Muck	Very much the same sort of person.
lair	A fellow who not only brags a lot, but generally dresses in very loud clothes in order to attract attention to himself.
laired up	What you wear when you 'lairise'. Top priority is to draw attention to yourself.
lairise	To act like a lair ... typical activities include 'mooning' a busload of tourists or doing 'wheelies' up and down Main Street.

larrikin	A young, mischievous male; a lout or hoon.
lash out	To go on a wild spending spree. 'I think I'll lash out on a brand new suit today.'
lav	Outdoor toilet. Abbreviation of 'lavatory' or 'lavvy'.
left footer	Anyone of Roman Catholic persuasion. 'I think he kicks with the left foot.'
leftie	Anyone who has socialist ideals.
lippie	Yet another example of the great Australian penchant for shortening words ... if you got lipstick, well done!
liquid amber	Beer.
little house	Sorry, Michael Landon — out here, it's the toilet!

lash out

loaf I really had to use my loaf to write this tome. Loaf is shortened from 'loaf of bread' which, of course, rhymes with head!

lob Not one of my better tennis shots! In Australia, if you 'lob in' on someone, you arrive unexpectedly.

lolly A sweet or candy.

lolly, do your When you 'do your lolly' out here, you have become very angry and have started shouting and raving.

doing your lolly

looney bin Mental asylum.

loop the loop Rhyming slang for soup, of course!

luv Often used as a substitute when you can't think of a woman's name. 'G'day luv, nice day eh?' 'Sure is, mate!' (She obviously can't remember his either!)

mozzie

mag — To indulge in idle conversation.

mail — Inside information. If you can manage to obtain some good 'mail' about a racehorse, you're home and hosed!

makings — 'The makings' are the ingredients you require to roll your own cigarettes: tobacco and cigarette papers.

mate — A friend, frequently used as a form of address. 'G'day mate, 'ow yer goin'?' 'Orright?!'

matilda — A bedroll generally carried by nomadic bushmen who walked or 'waltzed' around Australia looking for work. Hence the song, 'Waltzing Matilda', written by Banjo Paterson.

Melbourne Cup   Australia's best-known horse-race. So famous in fact, that in its state of origin, Victoria, Melbourne Cup day (the first Tuesday each November) is declared a public holiday.

Mick   Anybody of Irish descent or of Roman Catholic persuasion.

Mickey Mouse   Rhyming slang for 'grouse', excellent.

milk bar   A corner shop selling milk, bread, cigarettes, lollies and groceries.

missus   Your wife. In my case, a missus as good as a mile. GROAN!

mockers   If you 'put the mockers' on something, you are hoping bad luck will befall it. A bit like your average jinx.

moleskins   Robust trousers worn by Australian stockmen to prevent chafing while on horseback, and even more useful for preventing 'velour burn' on yuppie Range Rover drivers.

Melbourne Cup

Monday-itis

mollydooker	A left-hander. Personally, I'd give my right arm to be ambidextrous!
Monday-itis	That dreadful feeling of lethargy generally felt first thing Monday mornings at work after a famous Aussie weekend ... You are permitted to get it on a Tuesday as well!
moniker	Name. 'So, what's your moniker, mate?'
mooning	The act of dropping your trousers and exposing your buttocks in public.
moosh	Your mouth, your gob, your cake-hole!
motherless	Utterly, completely hopeless. 'He came stone motherless last in the race!'

mozz   Very similar to 'mockers'. When you put the 'mozz' on someone, you are hoping they'll screw up.

mozzie   Abbreviation of mosquito (of course!).

muck   Used in various forms. If you spend your week-ends just 'mucking about', it means pottering around doing nothing of consequence. On the other hand, if you 'muck' something up, you've just screwed it up . . . probably because someone put the mozz or the mockers on ya! Oh yeah — it's also something you can step in, e.g. dog's muck . . . yuk!

mudrunner   In horse-racing parlance, a mudrunner is a horse which revels in wet, heavy conditions.

munga   Another term for food or, as you guys say, grub!

muso   Short for musician. There is a myth that Aussie musos drink a lot, hence the old M.C.'s gag: 'The band is working under great difficulty tonight . . . they're all sober!'

mystery bag   A sausage. So named because you never know what your friendly butcher puts in them. Fear not though . . . they're quite edible!

mystery bag

nappies

name-dropper   Anyone who pretends to be a personal friend of the rich and famous. 'As a matter of fact, I was talking to Paul Hogan over dinner just the other night!'

nappies   Diapers. Napkins. Basic juvenile equipment.

narkie   Irritable, short-tempered.

never-never (1)   A term describing the most remote and isolated areas of Australia's inland desert.

never-never (2)   If you've just bought a stereo outfit on hire-purchase, you have bought it on the 'never-never'. It means either you never-never seem to be able to pay the interest or you never-never make a payment. We have a lot of 'occasional furniture' at home. We only ever make 'occasional' payments.

Niagaras

Abbreviation of 'Niagara Falls' which is rhyming slang for balls. If you get kicked in the 'Niagaras' it certainly makes your eyes water. Even worse if you're a bloke!

nick

If something is in 'good nick', it's in very good condition. If this dictionary sells well, my bank account will be in good nick! Then, I'll be able to 'nick off'.

nick, in the (1)

Quite simply, this means you are naked. Which begs the question: 'If naked aliens ever landed here, how would we know what NOT to look at!?'

Noah

nick in the (2)   To be in gaol.

nick off   To my villa in the south of France. When you 'nick off', you go away. It is quite acceptable to tell someone to 'nick off' if they are annoying you. Sort of like 'Scram!'

niner   Very popular at Aussie parties. It's a nine-gallon keg of beer which hardly ever sees the night out!

nineteenth hole   The bar at your favourite golf club.

Noahs   Abbreviation of 'Noah's ark' which is rhyming slang for shark ... but you knew that − dincha!

noggin

Your head or a glass of beer. Use your noggin when you come out here and have a couple of noggins with the locals! Confusing isn't it!

no-hoper

A person who is an abject failure at everything they turn their hand to.

non compos

Abbreviation of Latin phrase, *non compos mentis*, which means you are close to unconsciousness due to over-indulgence in alcohol. Have you noticed how many alcohol-related words there are in this book so far?

nong

An idiot or foolish person.

noodle

Your head ... very similar to your noggin. If you were using your noodle you'd know that!

norks

Slang term for women's breasts.

north and south

Rhyming slang for mouth.

no worries

Expression used to instil confidence in what probably is a very worrying situation. Often used by tradesmen, accountants and politicians.

O.S.

ocker
Your typical, uncultured, chauvinistic Aussie male. He generally likes his beer, sport and women ... in that order!

oldies
A term generally used to describe one's parents. 'I might spend an hour with the oldies this weekend.'

once-over
If you give something the 'once-over', you have just given it a cursory perusal. Sometimes we like to go to the beach to give some of the sheilas the once-over ... and of course they're doing the same to the blokes!

one-armed bandit
A poker machine ... very popular in Sydney clubs.

ocker

on ya

No, not a strange Eastern philosophy but an abbreviation of the term 'good on you' ... which means 'well done!'

ooroo

Just another way of saying goodbye!

open slather

Unrestrained activity.

optic

Abbreviation of the term 'optic nerve' which is rhyming slang for 'perve'. You generally perve at the same beach where you give sheilas the once-over!

order of the boot

Not exactly an honour you like to have bestowed on you. It means you've just been fired.

O.S.

Part of the great Australian penchant for trivialising any significant experience. One never goes overseas, one goes O.S., or O.T. (over there), or F-One J-One (Fiji), or N.Y.N.Y. (New York).

order of the boot

outback   What we Aussies call the desolate heart of Australia, or any remote part of the country for that matter.

Oxford scholar   Rhyming slang for 'dollar'. We all love Americans 'cos they spend lots of Oxfords whenever they come here.

Oz   Our abbreviated affectionate term for this great country of Australia!

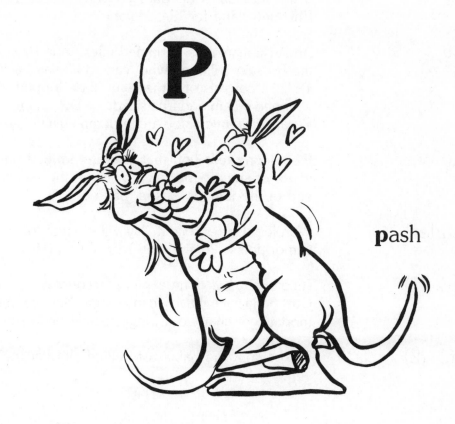

pash

paddywhacking   Spanking.

pants man   A man who fancies himself as a bit of a Casanova.

paralytic   Absolutely, totally intoxicated, or so drunk you can't scratch yourself. In fact, I'm surprised you've read this far!

pash   Abbreviation of 'passion'. Something you do in the back row of the movies when you kiss and cuddle . . . It's always nicer if someone is with you at the time!

pasting   If your team has just copped a pasting, it has just been thrashed or beaten in a very thorough manner.

Pat

If you are on your 'pat', you are in fact alone. Rhyming slang for 'Pat Malone'.

pav

An Australian dessert named after Anna Pavlova, the Russian ballerina who 'carked it' way back in 1931. It consists of a meringue base topped with whipped cream and fruit salad ... Do not attempt to eat these unless you are undergoing a fat attack.

pay out

If someone tells you that you are an idiot and a waste of space, you have been on the receiving end of the famous Aussie 'pay out'.

pearler

Wonderful or excellent. My wife is real 'pearler'. C'mon folks ... she may read this!

perk (1)

A company car or an expense account is a 'perk'. Our politicians have many perks but we mere mortals get charged a fringe benefit tax on ours!

perk (2)

Throw up. 'The baby just perked all over me!'

too much pav

perve — Something to do at one of our many beautiful beaches. Essentially, it simply means to leer at the opposite sex in a lustful manner. People who indulge in this pastime are known as 'perves'. Feel free to perve on this literary masterpiece!

Picadilly — Rhyming slang for 'chilly'.

piddle — Something you feel like doing when it gets a little 'Picadilly'. It means urinate ... racey stuff, eh!

pike out — To back out of an arrangement or a deal.

piker — If you pike out, you have failed to contribute a fair share to a team effort.

pimp — Yes, we have those in Australia as well, but someone who tells tales on you is also called a pimp.

pinko — Someone who is a communist sympathiser.

pip — Nothin' to do with Gladys Knight. If someone gives you the pip in Oz ... they are causing you extreme annoyance.

pissed — Really drunk. In fact, 'pissed as a parrot'! There are many derivations of this word, most of them offensive.

pixies — If you are 'away with the pixies', you are 'off the air', in a state of daydreaming and not really with us.

plates of meat — Rhyming slang for 'feet'.

plonk — Really cheap wine. Legend has it that to manufacture this wine, you throw a bunch of grapes into the air and they generally come down 'plonk'.

poet's day — Our term for Friday. It's a great Aussie tradition on Fridays to Piss Off Early Tomorrow's Saturday. Sorry, forgot to tell you ... 'piss off' in this context means to leave suddenly.

pong

pom

Affectionate Australian term for anyone of British extraction. There are various explanations for the origin of the term, but the most likely theory is that the initials P.O.M.E. stand for 'Prisoner of Mother England', dating from convict days. This was later shortened to POM.

pong

A very unpleasant odour. Some literary experts have said this dictionary has a certain pong about it!

poofter

Offensive term for male homosexual, and in Oz you don't even have to be one to be called one!

pork and bean

Sorry guys, here we go again. Yet another offensive term for a homosexual. Rhyming slang for 'queen'.

port

A term used, principally in Queensland, for a suitcase. Short for 'portmanteau'.

posh — Something or someone regarded as very refined, elegant or first class. We have many posh hotels in Australia. I've never seen any 'cos they won't let me in!

possie — Something essential at the football or cricket is a good possie. Abbreviation of 'position'.

postie — Continuing the penchant for shortening and adding 'ie' to words ... may I introduce the postman?

prang — Our term for a car wreck. See also 'bingle'.

prawn — Yes, it is what Paul Hogan calls a shrimp and if anyone 'comes the raw prawn' with you, they are trying to deceive or dupe you. Your retort should be, 'Hey mate, don't come the raw prawn with me or I'll give you a knuckle sandwich!'

preggers — In the club. Up the duff. In the pudding club. Tummy full of arms and legs. Give up? Okay, you're pregnant.

prezzies — Something you receive at Chrissie time of course! (And when you're preggers!)

pub crawl — Calling in to one hotel bar after another until you are totally inebriated ... Ancient Australian tribal custom!

puke — See 'perk (2)'.

pull your head in — It's our quaint way of telling someone to mind their own business.

put one over — Very similar to 'coming the raw prawn'.

put-up — If something is a 'put-up' job, it's generally regarded as a premeditated deed planned in a devious manner.

Qantas

Qantas — The only 'Q' word in the English language without a 'u'. An acronym for Australia's international airline, from Queensland and Northern Territories Air Service.

quid — Formerly the slang term used for the pound (currency). Still in use today. 'She's made a few quid out of her business.'

quid

razz

rabbit on	Talk incessantly.
rack off	Go away. Scram! Leave my presence immediately. Nick off! Get outa my face. All those!
rag	A newspaper of little substance or quality.
rag trade	The clothing business – either selling or manufacturing.
raincoat	Not only something to wear when it's raining, but yet another euphemism for a condom.
rapt	It you are totally infatuated with someone, you are said to be rapt in him or her.
ratbag	A person who is a little on the eccentric side.

rattletrap   An old jalopy that obviously rattles a lot and is probably a death-trap as well.

razoo   A gambling chip ... if you haven't even got a 'brass razoo' you are said to be stony broke.

razz   To make fun of someone in a precarious situation.

reccy   Surveying an area for a film, or just checking out a particular area to become familiar with it. Abbreviation of 'reconnaisance'. 'We had a good reccy around the town last night!'

rack off, ratbag!

red light district

Seedy area inhabited by whorehouses and prostitutes, from the old days when a red light indicated a brothel ... I once stood outside one all night waiting for the red light to turn green!

reffo

Abbreviation for 'refugee'.

Reg Grundy's

Rhyming slang for 'undies' (underpants). Reg Grundy is Australia's best-known game show producer ... He once offered me a job compering 'What's that smell?'!

rego

No, not Reg's Irish cousin but an abbreviation for 'registration' ... used when referring to a rego sticker for your car.

rellie

Short for relative ... your mum (sorry, mom), dad, sisters, brothers, aunts, uncles, etc. are classed as 'the rellies'.

Richard

If someone has had the 'Richard', it's had the 'Dick' ... that is, it's totally wrecked or useless.

ridgie-didge

Another form of 'fair dinkum', meaning it's the true, genuine article.

righto

This is really just another way we Aussies say 'okay' ... Righto?

ring

A rather uncomplimentary term for your anus ... My uncle got shot in the ring while rabbit hunting. They never found the bullet hole!

ringer (1)

The fastest shearer in the shed. Quite simply, he runs 'rings' around anyone else.

ringer (2)

Anyone who is a 'dead ringer' actually looks just like someone else. People say I'm a dead ringer for Paul Newman ... I never deny it!

ring-in

Something or someone substituted for the real thing.

ripper
Exclamation expressing delight or excitement. 'You little ripper!' Also used as a description: 'We had a ripper of a party last night!'

rip-roaring
Something loud or tumultuous. In Australia we often have rip-roaring 'booze-ups'!

ripsnorter
Yet another term expressing delight and pleasure. 'We had a ripsnorting, rip-roaring, ripper of a time at the booze-up ... and all woke up with a ripper of a hangover!'

roaring
If your business is doing well, you are said to be doing a roaring trade.

robber's dog
A really ugly person is said to have a 'head like a robber's dog' ... (We are talking major 'bow-wow' here!)

A HEAD LIKE A ROBBER'S DOG!

robber's dog

Rock, the Well, that could only be Ayers Rock, right?

rock and roller Term used to describe a Rolls Royce.

rocket If you 'cop a rocket' from the boss, it means he or she has given you a good castigation.

rollie A hand-made cigarette, as in 'roll-your-own'.

roo Abbreviation for kangaroo.

roo bar No, not something a kangaroo gets during the mating season, you filthy beast! It's a metal frame fitted to the front of your car to fend off roos when driving through the outback ... some kangaroos in Australia are the size of 'The Refrigerator'! (I wouldn't like to hit him at 100 k.p.h.)

root In the U.S.A., this word is a verb meaning to shout encouragement. In Australia, however, it means to have sexual intercourse. Be very careful how you use it!

rooted So obviously, if something is rooted it is said to be tired or totally useless.

rort A deceptive scheme. People receiving social welfare benefits under false pretences are 'rorting' the system.

rotgut Cheap, nasty liquor that does exactly as the name suggests.

roughie A horse with long odds which has little or no chance of winning a race.

r.s. Something of inferior quality, initials for 'rat shit'. Now *that's* inferior.

rubbidy Shortened version of 'rubbidy dub', rhyming slang for 'pub'.

run-around   You are getting the run-around if someone is being evasive with you or fobbing you off.

run-in   A quarrel.

rust-bucket   A car riddled with rust. I think mine is — it just dissolved halfway through the car wash.

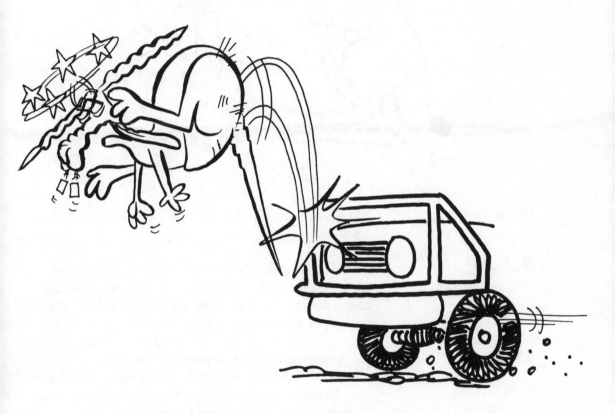

rooted by a run-in with a roo bar!

sheila

sack	When you are fired from your job, you get the 'sack'.
Sallie	Abbreviation for member of the Salvation Army. Also, 'Salvo'. Our suburb is so rich, the Salvos' band has a string section and a comedian who opens for them each night!
salute	As you constantly brush away flies from around your face, you are doing the great Australian salute. That's why we don't pull their wings off ... they're almost our national bird.
sambo	Certainly not the obvious ... it's a sandwich!
sandgroper	Anyone who lives in the state of Western Australia ... our biggest state.

sanger   Another sandwich!

sarky   Abbreviation for 'sarcastic'.

sausage roll   Rhyming slang for a 'goal' kicked during a game of Aussie Rules football.

scalper   Opportunist who buys and sells very quickly for a small profit, generally for a bit more than the official price. Usually football or concert tickets.

school   A group of people sitting around drinking and taking turns to buy each round is known as a school.

scone   Your head. Professors use their 'scone' a lot.

scorcher   We have a lot of these in Australia, especially in summer ... a very hot day. The last time New York had a scorcher, they asked the Statue of Liberty to put her arm down!

great Australian salute!

screamer

When one of our Aussie Rules footballers leaps high into the air to catch the football, he has just pulled down an 'absolute screamer' . . . then we really start barracking!

screamer

scrounge What the average wino does when he's searching through rubbish bins for food . . . or old copies of this book!

scrub Our term for bush country. 'I'm going up the scrub for my holidays.'

scrubber Young woman of questionable morals.

scunge A person who takes no pride in his or her personal appearance. Items of inferior quality are said to be 'scungy'.

semi Pronounced 'sem-ee' here, it's either a house attached to another on one side, or a semi-trailer, 'Breaker, breaker Big Daddy!'

send up To mock or satirise something.

serve Extreme admonishment. 'He copped a real serve from his boss when he got back late from lunch!'

shag (1) To be left 'like a shag on a rock' means to be totally forsaken or deserted.

shag (2) Yet another of our cute euphemisms for sexual intercourse. Cars used for this activity are referred to as 'shaggin' wagons' . . . cute, ay?

shaggers' back Back complaint humorously attributed to too much of the former activity. Obviously, you'll have to get a bigger car . . . or an apartment!

shandy A mixture of beer and lemonade . . . yecch!

shat off To be totally fed up or disappointed with something or someone.

sheila A woman. Of course, Australia has the grousest sheilas in the world.

shellacking — If your team has lost a game 200 to nil, it has just copped a 'shellacking' or severe beating.

sherbert — A beer.

shirt-front — In Aussie Rules football, a player who is downed by a head-on tackle from an opponent has just received a shirt-front ... they generally don't remember who did it till a few days later!

shirt-lifter — Not many of these blokes play footy in Australia. A male homosexual.

shirty — In a bad mood.

shitcan — To criticise someone or something quite vigorously. There are lots of other 'shit' words but my mum might read this book and get really 'shitty' about all the bad language.

short and curlies — Pubic hair. If someone has got you by the 'short and curlies' they have got you in a no-win situation. Ouch!

shout — When it's your turn to buy a round of drinks, it's your turn to 'shout' the school ... make mine a Harvey Wallflower, thanks!

shrimp — What we call prawns ... or anyone of puny stature.

sickie — A day taken off work because of illness. Sometimes we really *are* sick, but in Australia it's not a prerequisite as we're allowed about six 'sickies' a year ... Anyone for the beach!?

sin bin — Station wagon or panel van used at drive-in movies for getting to know one another ... another way to have fun at the drive-in is, when she goes to the toilet, shift the car.

skidlid — A bikie's crash helmet.

skinful	If you've drunk an awful lot of alcohol, you most definitely will go home with a 'skinful'.
skint	Bankrupt, broke . . . no money even!
skippy	A derogatory term for any Australian. Also the name of a popular T.V. series featuring a kangaroo called 'Skippy'. I think I may have eaten some kangaroo meat recently . . . I have this un-controllable urge to carry my kid around in my trousers!
skite	To brag, boast or show off.
sky rocket	Rhyming slang for 'pocket'.
slacker	Anyone who avoids toil.
slash	To urinate.
slipper	When someone is kicked during a brawl, they have just become a 'sink the slipper' victim.
slops	Another term for beer. A night 'on the slops' is a common pastime in Australia.
sly grog	Liquor sold illegally. This was very common in Australia when hotels were required to close at 6 p.m. This law was abolished in the early 1960s.
smart Alec	A know-all.
smart arse	A close relative of Alec.
smasher	A person who is very attractive to the opposite sex.
smell	A bloke who won't leave you in peace is said to be 'hanging around like a bad smell'.
smoko	A short time taken off work for a cigarette . . . might have one myself.

snag — A sausage ... see 'mystery bags'.

spag — Short for spaghetti, of course! Also, an offensive term used to describe people of Italian origin.

speed merchant — A petrol-head or fast driver.

spinebashing — The act of being stuck to your bed, hopefully asleep.

spit — When you spit in Australia you are generally very angry, so you 'spit the dummy', 'spit it out' or 'spit chips'.

sponger — Someone who lives off the efforts of others. A close relative of a bludger.

sprung

sport   Form of address that usually follows 'G'day!' Generally used between two guys when they can't remember each other's names.

sprung   If you come home and catch the milkman in bed with your wife, you have just 'sprung' them. 'Oh my gosh! It's your husband! Where's the back door!' 'We haven't got one!' 'Well, where would you like one!?'

spud   A potato. 'Ma, it's making eyes at me!'

spunk A good-looking, sexy guy or gal. Dolly Parton, for instance ... now, she's a great-looking sheila, aren't they!

squib Anyone who shirks an issue or situation in a cowardly manner.

squiz A quick perusal. I hope you take more than a squiz at this magnificent tome!

stack Something you do to your car in an accident. 'George stacked his car into a light pole last night!'

starkers Totally naked, or 'stark, raving mad', which means bonkers or crazy ... well, you'd have to be to walk around 'starkers', wouldn't you!

steak and kidney Rhyming slang for Sydney, capital city of Australia's most populous state, New South Wales ... about 4 million at last count.

stick Affectionate term for a person. 'She's not a bad old stick!'

sticks Somewhere well out of the city, the bush or the outback, in the general direction of 'Woop Woop'.

stickybeak A stickybeak is a person who likes to look into other people's business purely to satisfy their own curiosity.

sticky tape As the name suggests, tape you stick with (Scotch tape).

stiff cheese An expression of dubious origin but meaning 'bad luck'. You may say 'stiff cheddar' if you wish.

stirrer A person who delights in stirring up trouble then decamping when it gets out of control.

stretcher case   A sporting combatant who is carried from the field unconscious ... usually after a vigorous 'shirt-front'!

strewth   An exclamation of shock. 'Strewth! Did you see that shirt-front!'

strides   See 'daks'.

Strine   What this book 'issorlabowt'! Once you master the Aussie dialect, you'll be talking 'Strine' ... lazy corruption of 'Australian'.

stubby   A rotund little beer bottle. 'Get a few indyah when youse arrive, orright?!'

stuck-up   If you are a vain, conceited sort of person ... in Australia, you will be accused of being 'stuck-up' or 'up yourself'.

stuffed   If you are stuffed, you are either tired, full of food, or totally out of luck. However, if someone tells you to 'get stuffed', take umbrage ... you have just been told to go forth and multiply.

stuff-up   A bit like your average 'screw-up' or failure. There are only two things in life that have made me a failure ... bad luck and a distinct lack of talent!

stumps   Apart from our most famous one, the mythical 'Black Stump', stumps are three little sticks with bails on top at either end of a cricket pitch. It's every bowler's dream either to knock a batsman's bails off or to rattle his stumps! It means he's just got a 'wicket', which is like a pitcher striking out a batter in baseball.

suss   Abbreviation of 'suspicious'. Anything of dubious quality or origins is said to be 'a bit suss'. And if it is, you 'suss it out', which means check it out.

swag

Wandering bushmen, 'swagmen' or 'swaggies' carry all their belongings rolled up in a blanket. This is called a swag ... C'mon now, where are you going to find a supermarket trolley 1000 kilometres out in the bush?!

Sweet Fanny Adams

Our quaint way of saying 'nothing'. If you really want to drive home the point you could say, 'I came home from the track with sweet F.A.!' Which can also mean something else, if you're into swearing!

swipe

When you steal something, you are said to have swiped it ... or knocked it off or pinched it.

swy

If you visit a casino in Australia, enjoy a game of 'two-up' or 'swy'. This betting game, which involves throwing two coins up in the air and betting on which sides will fall uppermost, is also played illegally in what are known as 'two-up schools'. It is arguably the fairest form of gambling in existence today!

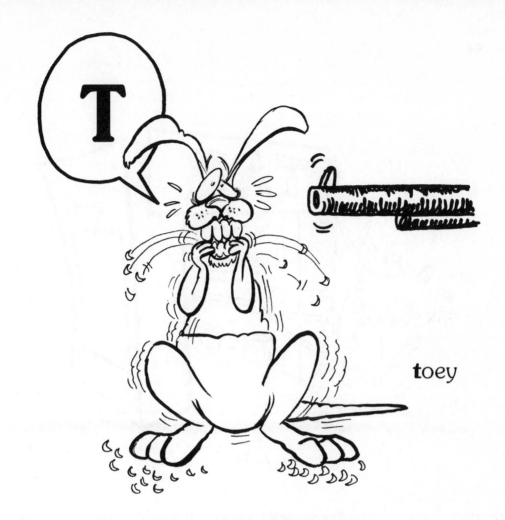

toey

ta	What the average Australian bellboy will say when you tip him. It simply means 'Thanks'.
T.A.B.	He'll probably take his tip to this place and place a bet on a horse. T.A.B. are the initials of our government-run Totalisator Agency Board betting shops.
Taffy	Anyone who comes from Wales, Great Britain.
tailor-made	Any cigarette that comes in a packet and is made by a machine. It is quite acceptable to ask a bloke for a 'tailor-made fag' without 'copping a bunch of fives'.
tarting-up	A cheap way of embellishing a building or a body for a quick sale. Buyer beware!

T.A.B.

ta ta	Pronounced 'tatt-tah', it doesn't mean you've said 'Thanks!' twice . . . you've just said 'Goodbye!'. If you are going on a trip, you are going 'ta ta's' . . . I don't believe I'm writing this!!
taxes	See 'highway robbery'.
tea leaf	Rhyming slang for 'thief'.
tear-arse	To travel rapidly. Young blokes like to tear-arse around in their cars.
telly	Abbreviation of 'television'. Sit in front of it long enough and you'll finish up with telly-belly!
thick	A stupid person is said to be 'as thick as two short planks'. My uncle Wilbur is so thick, he thinks the Supreme Court is where God plays tennis.

thick ear | If an Aussie male offers to give you a 'thick ear', duck! He's about to punch you and cause great swelling, especially around the ear area. If you say 'Yes!' to a 'thick ear', you are truly a 'thick' person!

thingummyjig | Anything you can't describe properly. Very handy for explaining car trouble to your mechanic ... 'I think it's that thingummyjig with smoke coming out of it that's causing the trouble' ... He'll probably have a 'thingummybob' to fix it!

thunder box | A toilet ... for obvious reasons!

tick | A short moment in time. 'Hang on a tick.'

tickets | To have 'tickets' on yourself is to be incredibly conceited. You ring Dial-A-Prayer and ask if there are any messages!

giving a thickhead a thick ear

tick off   A stern rebuke or scolding. 'The teacher gave young Johnny a good ticking off for his bad results.'

tiddly   Just a little intoxicated.

tight-arsed   Mean and miserly. 'That bloke's so tight-arsed, he wouldn't pull his wallet out of his pants unless they were on fire!'

tinnie   A cold can of beer. An absolute necessity at the footy or cricket . . . or even right now!

tinny   Lucky! 'I was really tinny at the casino last night.'

titfer   Abbreviation for 'tit for tat', rhyming slang for 'hat'.

toey   If you're eager or anxious about something you are getting 'a bit toey'.

togs   Swimming costume.

top-off   Someone who accidentally informs on another. In its malicious form, it's called 'dobbing'.

trammie   A conductor or driver of a tram. Melbourne is the only Australian city still using trams for general public transport.

trannie   Abbreviation for 'transistor radio'.

troppo   State of mild mental illness brought on by too much time spent in the tropics. 'Last time he was in Northern Queensland, he went troppo!'

trouble and strife   Rhyming slang for 'wife'. (Apt, that!)

true blue   Genuine, fair dinkum, spot on, etc. Also, the highest compliment you can pay an Aussie!

tucker   Food.

tuckerbag   Swagman's food bag ... what else?!

turn it up   Exclamation, basically meaning, 'Cut the crap!'

turn-up   An expression often used when something bobs up unexpectedly ... it is called a 'turn-up for the books'.

turps   Another term (and there are many more!) for alcohol. Abbreviation of 'turpentine'.

twig   Suddenly to realise or cotton on to something is to 'twig' ... Hopefully by now you've twigged to this funny language of ours.

two bob   Formerly two shillings, now twenty cents. Presently used to describe something cheap and unreliable. 'My car runs like a two-bob watch.'

two-bob lair   A fellow who dresses in cheap, gaudy clothes to draw attention to himself.

two-pot screamer   Anyone who gets drunk after only two pots (glasses) of beer.

two-up   A form of gambling involving spinning two coins into the air and betting whether they come down heads, tails or odds. See 'swy'.

umpie

u-ee	It literally means to do a U-turn while driving. We call it 'chucking a U-ee!'
um-ah	If someone is umming and ahhing, they are simply being indecisive. I *used* to be indecisive — but now I'm not so sure!
umpie	Abbreviation of 'umpire'. This poor maligned soul is never liked or correct with his decisions ... especially at the footy. Hence, the oft-shouted jeer, 'You bloody mug ump!'
umpteen	A very large indefinite number. 'This is the umpteenth time I've had to explain this word!'
underdaks	Underpants, shorts.
up a gum tree	In a hopeless situation.

u-ee

up the duff	Pregnant.
up the spout	You guessed it! . . . Pregnant again!
up yourself	Conceited, snobbish.
ute	Abbreviation of utility, an open-backed small truck.

underdaks

up the duff

Vegemite

vee-dub Abbreviation of 'vee-double-u', which is an abbreviation for Volkswagen, also known as a Vee-Wee. I broke my ankle in one at the drive-in, got my damn' foot caught in the glove-box!

Vegemite Trademark name for a black yeast extract used as a spread on toast and sandwiches. It also features in the hit song, 'Down Under' by Men at Work. Kraft, the manufacturers, claim it 'puts a rose in every cheek'.

vegies Vegetables.

verbal diarrhoea People who talk incessantly are said to have a bad case of it!

verbal diarrhoea

waterworks

wacker	A stupid nerd of a person.
wag (1)	A person prone to acting like an idiot in a good-natured way ... purely for laughs.
wag (2)	Our word for truant. I never 'wagged' school. My Dad used to walk with me every day ... he had to. We were in the same grade!
wake-up	If you're a 'wake-up' to somebody, you've suddenly realised what they're up to.
walkabout	A word used of Aborigines from a time when they would walk for miles in search of food, or go off to attend to ceremonial business. These days, if someone goes off without any particular destination in mind, they've 'gone walkabout'.

waltzing Matilda

walkover A very easy victory.

walk-up start Anyone who is easily conned is known as one of these.

waltzing Matilda From our most nationalistic song, it means wandering (waltzing) the countryside as a tramp, carrying your possessions wrapped in a blanket (Matilda). Believe it or not, this song can be a real tearjerker for any Australian abroad.

wanker A bloke whose stupidity is only exceeded by his over-inflated opinion of himself. You can see these guys coming a mile away!

war paint Cosmetics, generally applied by ladies before they go out searching for male scalps!

Warwicks Originates from Sydney racecourse, Warwick Farm. It's rhyming slang for 'arm'. On a hot day we all get a bit 'Alma Shetty' (sweaty) under the 'Warwicks'!

waterworks, turning on the A self-induced fit of crying, generally perpetrated by devious women to elicit sympathy. Can occur in men wearing underpants that are too tight!

wanker

wee-wees
What a child does when it goes 'toy-toys' for a 'pee-pee'.

wellies
Abbreviation of 'Wellington boot', more commonly known as gumboots or gummies.

whacko
Exclamation of delight. An extension of this is 'Whacko-the-diddle-oh!' ... silly, isn't it?

whack up
Something bank robbers do with their ill-gotten gains ... divide up or share equally.

whale into
Assault. 'He whaled into him with vicious left and right uppercuts.'

wharfie
One who works on wharves; a stevedore.

wheelie
The act of spinning your tyres and leaving on the road an amount of rubber equal to the density of your own brain.

whip around
A spontaneous collection of money for workmates about to leave your organisation, or for somebody down on their luck.

whopper
A gigantic lie.

wobbly
If you 'throw a wobbly', you have just lost control of your senses for a few moments of anger, out of frustration.

wog
Indefinable, harmless germ that incapacitates you for a day or so. It is a very common cause of 'sickies' in Australia. It is also an offensive term for anyone who hails from Central or Southern Europe ... However, it is quite acceptable to explain to your boss that you didn't come to work yesterday, because you were in bed with a wog! Wags in your office *always* chorus, 'What was his name?!'

wonky

After someone has slugged you and you start staggering around in a dazed state ... you're a 'bit wonky'.

wood duck

An easily fooled person ... easily picked off, just like a wooden duck in a shooting gallery.

wooden spoon

Non-existent prize for coming last in a competition.

Woop Woop

Fictitious location, generally used to signify the farthest, most remote areas. 'He lives a long way out ... in the back of Woop Woop somewhere.' Believe it or not, this word is in common usage!

wowser

Someone who neither drinks nor smokes, and doesn't believe in anyone having a good time ... their New Year's Eve parties always finish at about 10 p.m.!

write-off

If you bingle your $2000 car and cause $2500 damage to it ... it's a write-off.

X-out

ex   Term used to describe your ex-wife or husband.
                             'Darling, I would like you to meet my ex!'

X-out   To get rid of, or to erase someone or something.

ex

yarn

yabbie	Australian crayfish found in freshwater dams and creeks.
yahoo	Loudmouth, uncouth youth or person. Generally they accompany their entrance with the shout of 'Yahoo!'
yakka	Hard work — also the trademarked brand name of workers' overalls.
Yank tank	Large American car.
yap	Idle conversation. 'He just sat around yapping with his friends all day!'
yarn	A story, usually of adventure and usually very long.

Yarra

The river that flows through Melbourne in the state of Victoria. It's so muddy, people from other states claim it's the only river in the world that flows upside down ... Very hurtful that!

yobbo

A close cousin of a 'yahoo', generally of limited mental capacity, with a big beer belly.

yonnie

A stone or a pebble, ideal for 'chucking'.

you'll keep

An empty threat generally made when you can't think of a clever retort. Other expressions in such emergencies include: 'Oh Yeah!', 'Up yours!', 'Get stuffed!', 'In yer boot!' And if all else fails: 'I hope your chooks turn into emus and kick your dunny down!'

youse

Pronounced 'yewse'. This word is used to indicate more than one person. 'See youse all later!' (But not until you've read the next page!)

yabbie

Yarra

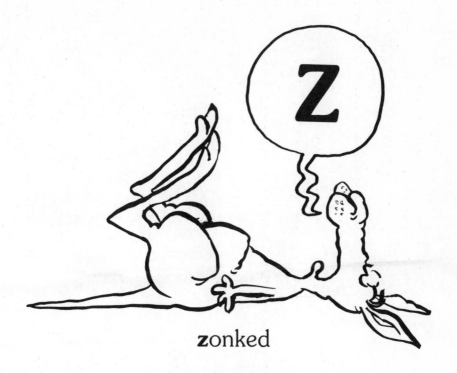

zonked

zack	Formerly a sixpence, now a five-cent piece.
zed	The way we pronounce the 26th letter of the alphabet.
zizz	A short nap, derived from the zzz's that you always see in cartoon strips.
zonked	A self-induced state of semi-coma, brought on by either a three-hour lunch, a day at the cricket, question time in Parliament or, Heaven forbid, a day at the office!